The
Italian
Therapy
Job

A Travel Diary

MIKE FOX

AuthorHouse™ UK
1663 Liberty Drive
Bloomington, IN 47403 USA
www.authorhouse.co.uk
Phone: 0800 047 8203 (Domestic TFN)
+44 1908 723714 (International)

This book is printed on acid-free paper.

ISBN: 978-1-7283-9562-3 (sc)
ISBN: 978-1-7283-9561-6 (e)

Library of Congress Control Number: 2020903093

Print information available on the last page.

Published by AuthorHouse 02/20/2020

author HOUSE®

The Italian Therapy Job: A Travel Diary

Contents

Preface

My wife Sylvia has a condition known as Parkinson's disease. This affects her mobility and the associated medication sometimes influences her moods, but never her motivation. She is a fighter and does her level best to keep the condition at bay. Most of the time, she has to use a wheelchair when she is out and about. In 2016 we travelled across North America, an adventure which formed the basis of my first book *Travelling by Road, Rail, Sea, Air (and Wheelchair) in North America*. This travel experience proved beyond doubt that where there is a will and a way, distance is no object, even for people with Parkinson's and who are wheelchair users. We also discovered that in many ways, the world is a kind place, and we had many pleasurable experiences (one verging on the miraculous) on that voyage of discovery.

Shortly after we returned from our trip to the New World, Sylvia and I learnt of the existence of the European Parkinson's Therapy Centre. It is located in the small Italian resort town of Boario Terme, in the foothills of the Alps in the north of the country. It lies not much more than a stone's throw from Milan, but far enough distant to seem like a million miles away from that metropolis. For us, this was a combination of visiting a (potentially) beautiful place (which it turned out to be), but also an opportunity for us to learn more about the disease or condition, with a possibility, so the information over the internet informed us, of encouragement and self-improvement in adjusting to and to an extent manipulating Parkinson's to Sylvia's advantage.

But in reality we knew very little about what we were letting ourselves in for. No one we personally knew had been there. It was a step into the unknown. But at least it had the makings of a fun holiday, and we even succeeded in persuading Sylvia's sister, Janet, a retired teacher from several years in Hong Kong, who is known to relish the odd adventure or two, to come with us and be part of the experience. So in June 2017, the three of us set off from Devon in the UK, and our two weeks in Italy are chronicled in this book.

GETTING STARTED

It's a long journey by car to Stansted Airport on crowded roads, especially on the M5 motorway. The South West of England where we live may be popular with tourists, but there is a lot of traffic trying to escape the region on this late spring Saturday. The congestion is exacerbated by a car crash on the M5 near Bridgwater. Later on, flashing blue lights appear in my rear mirror on the M4 somewhere past Reading; a motorcade, driven at speed, with four outriders on motorbikes, waving cars off the outside lane, followed by four cars, including a couple of Range Rovers, leave us for dead and are soon out of sight. Is this the Prime Minister on the move?

We come off the M4 just after its elevated section in West London, and negotiating the North Circular Road makes a pleasant change from motorway driving. We are aware of driving through distinct communities in this segment of London, including Indians near Wembley and Jewish rabbis trying to cross the road at Mill Hill. I still get a buzz seeing the diverse ethnicities and cultures which make such a contribution to the metropolitan character of Greater London.

Everything runs smoothly until we drive into the village of Takeley in the county of Essex and start looking for our airport lodge. I stop in the car park of a public house called the Four Ashes to ask for directions. The chatting stops as the regulars eye me up and down through a pall of smoke. No one seems communicative in the wall of silence. After I ask for directions, someone silently points along one of the roads leading away from the cross roads. It turns out to be the opposite direction, and twenty minutes or so later, we drive into the Stansted Airport Lodge and meet a much friendlier face upon entry.

The receptionist is a Polish guy called Marek, and I remember him from last time we used this place, en route to the Faroe Islands. Marek tells us we have two double rooms. When Janet informs him that we only require one double and one single room, he replies: "No problem; in the night I come into your room!" It's good to know that Marek's humour hasn't diminished in three years.

We go out in the early evening for a meal in a nearby hotel, which is a short wheelchair ride for Sylvia back into the village. We pass a few cottages which appear to date from Tudor times. Cars parked over the pavement force us at one point to wheel Sylvia into the highway. Back at the Stansted Airport Lodge, I put the European Cup Final on the TV and watch Ronaldo score his zillionth goal in Real Madrid's 4-1 win over Juventus. I shed a small tear for Buffon, the Juventus goalkeeper, who has now been on the losing side in all six finals he has played in. Then, it's an early night.

Sunday 4 June

THE JOURNEY TO ITALY

Despite going to bed early, Sylvia has had a difficult night. The hotel room at the Stansted Airport Lodge is OK, but it's difficult for Sylvia, as there is nothing to hold onto along the walls, and she is struggling with her movement right now, as many Parkinson's sufferers do. There is breaking news on my mobile of an act of terrorism on London Bridge, with at least six people dead. Stansted is unlikely to be directly affected, me thinks.

We manage to make breakfast at the Lodge, which advertises the slightly eccentric times of 03:00 hrs to 09:30 hrs, presumably reflecting the patterns of flight departures from Stansted. There's little milk or orange juice left in the dining area, but our self-service breakfast is a relaxed affair, with no one else around. I park my car in a shady area by some trees before our taxi driver picks us up for the short ride to the airport. Interestingly, he warns us about the Four Ashes pub, where we had our unwelcoming experience yesterday. I'm glad it wasn't just me then.

I experience the 'wow' factor as I arrive at the superb, iconic terminal at Stansted designed by Sir Basil Spence. Our chatty wheelchair pusher says she came over to the UK from France six years ago with her mother who is from Chad. She is hoping to visit her mother's country for the first time next year. She even retrieves our £1 coin from our luggage trolley; how considerate is that?

There is a slight spot of bother at the check-in desk. The police are called to speak to a guy, who is saying to them in a loud voice: "I want to go to Morocco!" But it's none of my business and I quickly move on.

Our second assistant is Chris, who announces himself as our 'dodgy' wheelchair driver; he's been doing the job for only four weeks and is still enthusiastic. As usual with wheelchair access, we secure a quick route through and onto the plane, where we are seated at the front, with a little more leg room.

I sit next to an amicable Italian who says he has just celebrated his eightieth birthday party in London. The plane fills up to capacity, as a continuous stream of disgruntled Juve supporters files past us and along the aisle. The guy next to me turns out to be an Inter fan. He says in quite a loud voice that he is so happy at the result: "Juve have given us so much sh*t over the last few years, and they only win because they are a bunch of robbers – I am so happy!" There are glares from the throngs of Juve fans boarding the plane, and I am wondering whether we are going to have a punch up any minute now.

I am distracted from the thoughts of disharmony on the plane by great views of Dover and its magnificent harbour through the scattered clouds. It's a busy port, with several ferries coming and going. The Channel looks very narrow from our grandstand view and soon we are flying over Calais. Sometime later, the Alps come into view, but they are mainly obscured by clouds, with the occasional icy, rocky peak protruding through the cotton wool. The noise of a single screaming child from somewhere near the centre section of the plane is largely drowned by the not inconsiderable noise of the aircraft.

My 80 year old Italian friend in the next seat turns out to be friendly and helpful. He teaches me the Italian for "no problem" ("non che problema"), which he says you can use generally in Italian society – but not, he says, if the hotel staff tell you that they have given you the wrong room, or worse, no room at all; then it is a "grande problema!"

Milan Bergamo Airport is small and easy to negotiate. It's located some way out of Milan, with a view of a solid line of high hills on the other side of the runway, set in pleasant rural surroundings. We are collected at the airport by Michaela, the young driver of a people carrier, charged with getting us to our hotel. The journey of an hour or so takes us through a mixture of forested valleys, a few quarries and pockets of heavy industry and the sandy-shored Lake Endine with its thriving industry of pedal boats.

Michaela points out her home village of San Antonio. It comprises a small cluster of dwellings, perched precipitously high on the slopes of the mountainous ridge to our right. She asks me if I have been to Italy before, and where. When I mention Naples, she says that in the south, it is a different land with different people. "Does that mean there are two Italys?" I ask. "Exactly, that's it!" she replies.

The small settlement of Boario Terme is a spa town in a valley between a line of steep, craggy, limestone mountains to the north-west and the less dramatic, but still high, forested slopes of the uplands to the south-east. Our hotel, the Hotel Diana, is a five minute walk (or ten minutes if you walk slowly) from the therapy centre, located above the spa. Our hotel is family run, with a pleasant, homely atmosphere, and the staff are keen to welcome us. Our bedroom window looks out across a small, enclosed patio garden, complete with a fountain, beyond which is a backdrop of forested hills. It's perfect. I hope the sound of the running water doesn't keep me awake all night.

Our first meal at the hotel is superb, except for the serious risk that I might put on a lot of weight. We then ask one of the reception staff, who refers to herself as 'Mama' (and I think she is the one who actually runs the hotel as the matriarch) for directions to the European Parkinson's Therapy Centre, where Sylvia will be put through her paces for the next fortnight. She insists on walking with us through the town as far as a ramp, so as to avoid a flight of steps.

The therapy centre is situated in the centre of town on the main thoroughfare, just beyond a set of traffic lights, as 'Mama' had told us. The therapy centre occupies part of a famous wellness centre, next to a contemporary extension, its setting augmented by a water feature. Most of this complex is the actual spa that gives the town its name and raison d'être ('*Terme*' is the Italian for 'spa', where the thermal waters seep through from the surrounding limestone rocks). Next to the buildings an area of parkland stretches away to the north. At first glance, as seen through the glass doors, the entrance to the main building looks like a stage set for the Temple of Zeus, but this could be my imagination working overtime in response to the atmospheric lighting effects inside the building. The place has a resort feel to it, a kind of Italian version of Buxton in England.

It is clear, as we look around and upwards from the main street, that Boario Terme occupies a strip of relatively flat land, constrained within a steep-sided valley. High, rocky crags to the north-west are near vertical in places with some vegetation squeezed into narrow gullies. On the opposite side of the valley, is a line of thickly wooded slopes. We are located in the Camonica Valley, which makes its way up into the Alps to the north-east of Boario Terme.

Then it's back to the hotel for quick drinks (tea for the ladies, coffee for me). At ten o'clock I notice that the water fountain in the patio garden beneath our bedroom has been switched off; the silence is golden.

THE INITIATION

Sylvia and her sister Janet at the Thermal Gardens

Come on Sylvia!

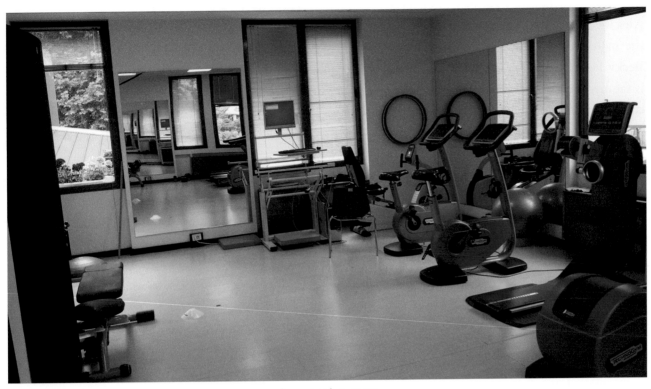

Impressive gym

More work in the gym

A combination of the fountain, my mobile alarm, a barking dog and the sound of church bells wakes me from a deep sleep. We had thunder during the night, and at one point, lightening lit up the room.

We make it through the rain to the therapy centre in time for our initial session. Silvia the psychotherapist welcomes us to the centre and explains its ethos. She says the centre, which was established by an English guy called Alex Read, has a different approach to the treatment of Parkinson's compared to what is sometimes referred to as the 'mainstream', but it is an approach that is supported by Michelle Hu, one of the UK's leading neurologists, Becky Farley, a leading American researcher and a number of other American and English practitioners. It is family-oriented and has a '360 degree' emphasis, meaning that all aspects of the Parkinson's condition are considered important and need to be addressed.

Around 7-8 people per week come here for treatment, with the figure increasing during the summer. In particular, the centre's 'four pillars' of Parkinson's are a helpful framework for treatment and therapy: these are medicine; physiotherapy; lifestyle; and psychology – all are important and in the view of the centre, none can be ignored. It is unique in many ways which is probably why so many non-Italians find their way here too.

Silvia explains that the reality is that everybody has a neuro-degenerative condition; the key difference with Parkinson's sufferers is that the level of dopamine in the brain depletes at a faster rate than in the 'normal' population. One of the principal messages Silvia conveys to us is that Parkinson's limits but doesn't destroy our life, and in this sense it is not like cancer or Alzheimer's. We are not victims, she says; we have a choice, and in some ways it can open up new opportunities. Some of the statistics she presents are stark: 80% of Parkinson's sufferers don't seek help; clinical depression affects sufferers at a rate of about 50%, which is greater than the average population and 10% think their life is over at diagnosis. These may be the statistics from the Western World, but then Parkinson's is mainly a Western disease.

Silvia then talks about the second pillar – physiotherapy – and its value. Exercise can increase our neuro protection; it can even increase dopamine levels in a natural way.

Then we come to the part of the presentation that really appeals to me. Silvia talks about accepting that we are on the slow train and the importance of enjoying the ride. It's a different train from the Japanese bullet train for example, but, hey, we can enjoy the ride and we can get to see different views. I never thought we would be talking about trains at a Parkinson's therapy centre!

Sylvia is given a pedometer and it will be interesting to see how far she has come (literally) over the two weeks of the course. Silvia, the psychotherapist, invites us to forget all we know about Parkinson's and come with an open mind; relax and enjoy our time here; live each day at a time; and reflect and apply the exercises and principles from the course.

The discussion turns to eating and then on to lifestyle. On the subject of stress, Sylvia says that she picks up on other people's stress, and it's difficult to see how this can be avoided. Sylvia is encouraged to carry on with her Pilates, which reinforces core muscles. The importance of taking medication at least an hour after meals is emphasised. And we are told that it is not good to have protein at lunch near to the time we take medicines, because it affects the effectiveness of the medication, something we had not realised before.

One of the expectations of the therapy course is that Sylvia will walk more, and her pedometer readings will be interesting in this regard. In the afternoon, after we go back to the hotel for a good but large lunch, Sylvia starts her sessions with her 1:1 physio, a young lady by the name of Agata. Almost her first words to Sylvia are: "I will push you, but please don't hate me". Sylvia is asked to walk completely unaided, up and down a corridor. Agata comments, and the short video highlights this, that there is a big asymmetry in Sylvia's movement (I think that means she has a bit of a wobble), and stresses the importance of regaining her symmetry.

Agata is also not impressed with Sylvia's ancient pair of trainers that she has brought with her, and suggests she changes into her newer ones. But the older pair does demonstrate the differential wear on Sylvia's feet. So she has to shift her balance to the left; well, that's the theory.

Then Sylvia is asked to walk round the gym for a six-minute period. *"Come on Sylvia!"* exhorts Agata, as Sylvia pounds round and round the gym. In the end, Janet, me and a few others join in the chorus of "Come on Sylvia!" Sylvia achieves 152 metres. We will see what happens when this test is repeated.

At the end of Sylvia's first session, we leave the centre, and to avoid the pouring rain, we delay our walk/trundle back to the hotel by stopping for a cup of coffee in a small café at the entrance to the spa. Then we risk getting soaked, as there seems to be no let-up in the rain.

The rain does clear, however, although the afternoon is still misty. I venture out for a walk on my own. I follow the railway as far as the single platform station of Boario Terme. A smart green diesel train arrives within minutes, and about 20 young African men say goodbye to a couple of their friends who board the train, amidst lots of embraces and handshakes. The train leaves and within minutes there is not an African face to be seen. I walk back to the hotel, past the contemporary Catholic Church of Our Lady of the Snow, with its slender but brutalist concrete bell tower, reminding me of the architecture of some UK fire stations. At 6:16 pm, the bells seem to chime forever, maybe to announce a church service.

On one of the walls back at the hotel, I study a huge and colourful map of the Camonica Valley, resplendent with contours. It confirms my hunch that the railway to the south of Boario Terme passes along the eastern shore of Lake Iseo, with a station at Sulzano. This is the place from where Silvia (the Psychologist) told us this morning that a local artist by the name of Cristo has constructed a golden 'floating pier', connecting the town to the island of Monte Isola, in the middle of the lake.

Over dinner at the hotel, we are given free tickets for a music concert in the gardens next to the spa. Sylvia and I decide to go along, and the rain by this time is only slight. We eventually discover a convoluted access ramp for the wheelchair.

There are not too many people attending what could be described as a tea dance. A dozen or so older couples are dancing to the sound of piped music, including a couple of ageing Lotharios, if that's not too harsh a term to use. We stick it for about an hour.

Sylvia's pedometer registers 1,445 steps and progress on Day 1 of the course has been good. I make a start on John Grisham's *Calico Joe* before bed.

CYCLING FOR VICTORY

Village of Sulzano

Island village of Peschiera

Contemporary fish art

Rain approaching Lake Iseo

Another wet day is forecast. We don't need to be at the centre until ten o'clock, so we enjoy a bit of respite after yesterday's exertions.

Agata starts Sylvia off with a series of what are termed 'power' exercises. The first of these – power up – is a stretching exercise. Agata shouts: "pay attention!", but this is an example of the difficulties in translation, as she merely means that Sylvia has to concentrate, rather than as a reprimand. Sylvia looks like she is swimming through air when she does this exercise. The second exercise – power twist – is done with a stick or baton, again with lots of stretching. In another exercise Sylvia is put through, she is slowly sitting up and slowly sitting down. It sounds easy but looks can be misleading. "When sitting, aim for the right!" instructs Agata. Then it's on to a hand cycling machine. "Speed up, Sylvia!" urges Agata. After this, it's onto the proper cycling machine, and Sylvia struggles a bit more.

But after all these gruelling exercises, Sylvia walks and there are distinct signs of improvement. She is definitely walking better, even after one day at the centre. There is logic to the exercises. The next instruction is for her to be placed on a couch doing stretching exercises, with her legs raised. Some of Agata's pressing on Sylvia's leg muscles looks painful from the other side of the gym. We invite Agata to come and work on Sylvia in England, but she says she gets married on 25 June, so I guess that's just about an acceptable reason for her not to jump ship and come to England.

It's time to relax over a drink in the entrance café. The lady serving us has good English. She says she also learnt French and Spanish at school, but she found the Spanish easier. "It must be the sangre latino!" she says. Janet talks about the possibility of starting her own Parkinson's centre in the UK, possibly based in Torquay.

The afternoon is free time for me. I take the 14:46 train to Sulzano. The rain has cleared; low lying cloud lingers half way up the sides of the surrounding mountains. A friendly lady from Moldova asks me if I am a tourist before catching a train in the opposite direction. My train comes into view, and it is a smart looking set of diesel multiple units. There is something stylishly Italian about it.

On the train, I ask the conductor for a return ticket to Sulzano, but they only issue singles for some reason. The train suffers the indignity of being overtaken by a bus at one point. Small villages perch improbably in the upper reaches of the mountains. They were farming villages at one time, but I wonder whether they are mainly inhabited by commuters these days. This must be the school train that I am riding; the kids on board make a lot of noise and commotion, but it seems pretty harmless to me. Maybe if my Italian were better, I would revise that opinion.

After 20 minutes or so, the train runs alongside the shore of Lake Iseo, plunging through a number of tunnels. I reach Sulzano after about 40 minutes. I leave the train and negotiate a couple of narrow passageways and emerge at a landing stage. Almost immediately, I board a ferry bound for the hilly island in the middle of the lake, which goes by the name of Monte Isola.

One of the reasons I have chosen to visit Sulzano is to see the golden piers that I have been told were built across the lake last year. But it quickly becomes apparent once the ferry has dropped me off on Monte Isola that the famous piers in golden wood were constructed for a limited exhibition for a month or so in June/July 2016. There is no sign of it now. But there is quite a lot of contemporary art on display along the lakeside walkway, including several stone fish, as I stroll along past cafes and small houses. I find myself in the middle of an English touring party with a predominance of Midlands accents, but not for long.

The buildings hugging the shoreline are mainly traditional and pleasant without being truly outstanding, and they extend back up the hill for a couple of storeys. But it's all very appealing. Several small power boats are idling in the slightly choppy water. The rain has now disappeared, although dark clouds hover close to the tops of the mountains, accompanied by the sound of distant thunder.

I buy a coffee at a small waterside café and to my embarrassment I discover that some of my small change is Canadian! Apart from a few noisy scooters, I find that sitting by the edge of the lake, drinking coffee here is a peaceful experience, with the only sounds emanating from the water lapping against the boats and a few garrulous ducks.

I make my way back to the ferry landing, complete with its real time information board. Even gas power is to be introduced to the island in a month's time according to the information boards. As I wait for the ferry to Sulzano, one guy, possibly in his mid-twenties, escorts his (considerably) older friend (who could be in his forties) who is patently completely drunk and for all purposes, dead to the world. But he isn't too noisy, and everyone in the ferry queue seems amused.

As the ferry draws near to the mainland, the thunder starts up again and the skies darken. Rain can be seen falling from the south and the temperature drops; great conditions to take a few photographs without (for the moment) getting wet. I walk briskly from the waterside to the shelter at the railway station, and I manage to beat the advancing rain by a few minutes; it is close, though. The clouds descend even lower and a church bell strikes five o' clock. Then the rain falls, and it is torrential; my fast walking has paid off. A lot of noisy birds seem to have a lot to say as the rain clatters onto the station roof.

The downside of rushing back to the station is a 40 minute wait for the train to Boario Terme. But the wait is not boring. I share the platform with one singing African man and one quiet African man. Then we are joined by the aforementioned guy and his drunken friend, who board a train for Brescia in the opposite direction. An old lady with a black headscarf, who looks as if she has come straight out of the Balkans, tries with difficulty to control a lively girl of primary school age, which includes giving her a few sharp raps on her leg with her walking stick. The girl continues to hide from her exasperated grandmother right up until the arrival of the train.

I spot a tiny island in the lake, just off the larger island of Monte Isola, which is dominated by a church with a tower, protruding above the cypress trees. Unfortunately, the view from the train is somewhat compromised by a large cement works and quarry on the opposite shore of the lake. The rain stops, as the railway veers away from the lake at the small town of Pisogne.

Back at the hotel, after another ample to large meal, which as ever is hugely enjoyable, we chat over coffee in the hotel bar, made even more relaxing by the background music of Jean Michel Jarre's *Oxygen*. Our waitress this evening says it is going to be "sun, sun, sun" tomorrow, and hopefully she is right. We are thinking of inviting Anja, a Swiss student who stayed with us as part of our family until a few weeks ago, to travel over to join us, maybe at Lake Garda on Sunday. I also ask Mauro at reception about train times to Verona, which the guide books rave over. We are too tired to venture out into the town, and retire to our rooms at 9:20pm.

STRETCHING AS WE NEVER KNEW IT

Our waitress was right, and it's a sunny day. Sylvia is also in fine fettle and walks about half way to the centre from the hotel, including climbing up a flight of steps.

Agata says it's time to activate the quadriceps. "Stretching is fundamental" she says. Some of it is also clearly painful, as Sylvia is put through her paces. It's more stretching exercises with a ball and then a towel under her knee. "You can do this at home!" enthuses Agata. Half an hour later, Sylvia is back on the bicycle.

Janet and I have been spectators up to this point. This abruptly changes. Agata takes the three of us into a room with wall mirrors and she gets us to do a set of power movements together – power twist, power rock and power step. I am castigated by Agata for not trying hard enough, but Sylvia is doing well, and her symmetry is better than yesterday. We have to touch our opposite knees – left hand to right knee; right hand to left knee. It sounds easy, but it's a killer after a while.

I get through to Anja on my mobile just before lunch, and we agree to chat later when she's not at school. She suggests meeting up at Lake Garda, which is a four-hour drive for her. Someone on reception at the hotel says we can get to Desenzano, on the shores of Lake Garda in two hours by train.

Our hotel has a delightfully secluded garden with a small fountain in one corner, plus five tables and chairs on a cobbled, stone surface, together with a few trees and plants; a cross between a garden and a patio. It is bounded on three sides by the hotel building and on the fourth by a high wall, maybe as high as five metres. The wall is covered by flowers protruding out of boxes and plants growing down the side of the wall. Above the wall, there is a view of some of the forested valley side, and on a good day like today there is blue sky punctuated by a few white clouds. The centre piece is a statue of a Roman lady, although I am reliably informed by the hotel 'Mama' that she is not Diana, whom the hotel is named after. This is the perfect place to get stuck into a good book, which I do, reading *The Trains now Departed* by Michael Williams.

After Sylvia's afternoon therapy, we follow the map to a riverside walk. But the map doesn't show the gradients, and there are quite a few of them, making pushing the wheelchair a real challenge. One narrow road has steep gradients plus sections with no footways, and with an uneven surface – a real challenge for the wheelchair pusher (me). An ancient, arched stone bridge comes into view, with an old church in the background. Both Janet and I burn off a lot of calories pushing the wheelchair in the hot, sunny weather. It is 27°C today, and it is forecast to rise to 33°C by Monday.

Anja rings me this evening; common sense has kicked in and she realises that she is in the middle of her A levels with several exams next week. So, sensibly, she thinks it is not possible to drive over and meet us for the day. I agree to send her a post card.

Sylvia is under the weather after another full day's exertions. She struggles with her movement at dinner, in the bar afterwards, and getting to bed. But we succeed in locating the anti-histamine tablets, so she at least should get a good night's sleep.

I develop a slight headache, in sympathy with Sylvia, due partly at least to the exposure to the sun all afternoon. We are in bed shortly after ten. Sylvia's ped counter has registered 2,365 paces.

THE THERMAL GARDENS

We both experience a good night's sleep. Over breakfast, one of the friendly members of the hotel staff indicates, using hand signals, that Sylvia has improved her walking. So it's not just our wishful thinking and there is a reason Agata does what she does.

At the centre this morning, Agata tells Sylvia that she has to walk to the gym from the reception, without using a stick. Sylvia starts on the walking machine, followed by a bridge exercise, where she shifts her body weight on the couch, bending her right leg and stretching more her left leg. Sylvia then lies on her side, knees bent, twisting her body, to the sound of Coldplay.

Janet and I are quietly sipping coffee in the entrance area to the thermal pool when an old man approaches us and shows us some paintings in a brochure. I am not sure whether he is the artist or a street vendor. He puts his glasses and his beaker on our table, and it looks like he's joining us for the duration. We don't encourage him, however, and he eventually takes the hint and goes away. Janet thinks that she accidently made eye contact with him, but I think he was determined to talk to us anyway.

The afternoon is free time, and we visit the extensive Thermal Park Gardens on what is a perfect, sunny afternoon, permeated by the ever-present smell of sulphur, which I don't find particularly unpleasant. We trade in Sylvia's pass for three free entry tickets, which seems like a good deal to me.

The main structure in the park is the Cupola Marazzi, which architecturally cuts a dash in a town which has a pleasant though undistinguished townscape. Next to the cupola is a semi-tented dance floor. A group is on stage churning out the Italian equivalent of Country and Western and over a dozen couples of indeterminate ages north of 60 are clearly entering into the spirit of things.

We walk away from the noisy dance floor and we are soon experiencing the quiet atmosphere of the park. The park is great at absorbing sounds and within yards the sounds of music and dancing are lost in the cool of the tall pine trees. We also catch glimpses in the far distance of the last remains of snow in the upper crevices in the mountains of the Camonica Valley, towards the Swiss border.

At the northern end of the park, there is a track which spirals and then shoots up the valley side, referred to in the information guide as an Alpine Coaster. But it stands in silence, with no thrills and spills to observe.

We spend some time enjoying the sights and sounds of the tea dance under the large canopy by the cupola. Janet remarks that all Italian men look the same, but do I believe her?

Back at the hotel, Sylvia and I read in the small garden. 'Mama' from reception comes into the garden soon after we sit down there and switches on the fountain just for us; a nice touch.

Sylvia has had a good day, but she tires after our substantial evening meal. Her ped count today is 1,221 paces.

Friday 9 June

ONE GENTLEMAN GOES TO VERONA

Amphitheatre and the Lady with Big Eyes, Verona

Verona street scene

Archaeological dig, Verona

Statue of Juliet

Verona Market

River Adige, Verona

Milan bound express

Ponte Pietra

Beautiful arch

It's been a bad night for Sylvia. She had very little sleep, and after breakfast I walk over to the centre to say that Sylvia will arrive late. Back home in the UK, it's also been a bad night for Theresa May, who has somehow managed to snatch defeat – or at least a hung parliament - from the jaws of a landslide victory in the UK General Election.

Our psychotherapist, Silvia, asks Sylvia, who has now turned up, about how she has felt about this week. Sylvia says she hasn't been able to sleep and is suffering from constipation (a common feature of Parkinson's). "But" she says "I am determined to improve and work on my timing for taking medication and improving my diet". Silvia says, referring to the 'four pillars': "your medication seems OK; on the physical side, Agata is proud of you, but you have to keep on improving; the psychological aspect is not a problem; regarding lifestyle, motivation is important, and we have a session to help with tying together the various strands". She also says the people at the centre love to receive feedback, e.g. through e-mails. Silvia then says, rather ominously: "Next week, we go to the second level".

At this point, mid-way through the morning, I bid farewell to the centre for the rest of the day and walk to the station, to catch a train to the city of Verona, which achieved worldwide fame through being the setting for the Shakespearian tragedy *Romeo and Juliet*. As I approach the station, I am hassled by a Romanian lady, who says she is desperate for money. I give her a euro, but she complains that this is not enough; she says she wants 2 euros. In the end I walk away.

I then experience a surreal moment. A guy approaches me on the station platform and asks me something in Italian. I am pretty sure that he is asking whether he can buy a train ticket at the station. I answer "Non, sul treno" ("no, on the train"). He replies "grazie" and walks away. It may have been brief (very brief), but I have just had a conversation in Italian; absolutely no English was used. I feel good.

Looking at the scenery from the train, just to the south of Darfo I notice a linear village straggling the mountainside, running along a road which appears to have been blasted out of the rock. Then there is a gap, near a deep gorge. I can't make out any bridge crossing this incision in the landscape, and then the linear village continues. I am left wondering what sort of link there is between these two mountain settlements, so near to each other but perhaps also so far apart in terms of access.

Further south, the train passes along the shores of Lake Iseo, and Monte Isola and of course, no floating piers. We pass many attractive houses, some with swimming pools, a couple of high density caravan parks and beautiful old churches with their ornate bell towers.

After leaving the town of Iseo with its carriage sidings, the train runs through a generally flatter landscape, past vineyards and arable fields, but there are a few hills and the scenery is pleasantly pastoral, if not quite on a par with Tuscany. Occasional tracks invitingly head into mysterious forests, which I will probably never have the opportunity of exploring.

Our single track branch railway joins the electrified main line just before I terminate the first leg of my journey at the industrial town of Brescia. The 'no smoking' signs on the platforms at Brescia are largely ignored.

My train to Verona is a Venice-bound express, which obligingly comes in on the opposite side of the same island platform where the train from Boario terminates. A 'no smoking' message comes over the inter-com system, first in Italian and then in English, when it says: "Smokers on the train will be persecuted" (!).

Despite the crowded train, I manage to catch a good glimpse of the expansive Lake Garda, near to Desenzano Station.

The next stop is Verona. It's around midday and it is sunny and hot, and I have a lot of walking to do if I am going to get a good look at this city. One of my first impressions is lots of cyclists, one of whom nearly knocks me down; I quickly become aware of the signs on the pavements, indicating dedicated cycle ways!

The railway station and its neighbouring bus station are fortunately built on the outside of the city wall, which here in its south-west section, is still intact and looking impressively thick. I walk through the Porta Nuova, the New Gate, which punches its way through the bastion of a wall which protected this city against all-comers in the Middle Ages.

I proceed along a wide thoroughfare, busy with pedestrians; it's as if the world and his dog has come to visit this famous city. Before long I walk into a huge square, the Piazza Bra, which forms the setting for the huge arena, dating from AD30, and looking almost every inch like the Colosseum in Rome. (It was the second largest in the Empire.) The scaffolding covering the gigantic structure might be necessary but clearly detracts from its grandeur. A huge stone head of a female, resting on the floor next to the arena, appears to be waiting to be hoisted into a permanent position. It seems to be scanning everyone who passes by through its enormous eyes.

I wander through the piazza and into a labyrinth of narrow streets, some revealing impressive courtyards, mainly protected from public access by sturdy gates. I consume a pizza at a pavement café in another, smaller square, before moving on to a real tourist honeypot, Giulietta's (or Juliet's) house. Crowds of tourists have converged on this iconic place. There is a golden statue of Juliet in the patio immediately in front of the house, which is adorned by the famous balcony which Romeo scales in Shakespeare's classic romantic tragedy. The statue is enjoyed with a lot of close, 'hands-on' attention from many tourists, and not exclusively male tourists either.

Moving on towards the river, I pass several statues lining the streets, including one of Dante, which reminds me that the street temperature seems to reaching inferno-like levels. I come across the banks of the River Adige, and my plan is to follow it as it meanders in an expansive curve before parting company with it at the Castelvecchio, Verona's ancient castle, and then heading back to the railway station. At the Ponte Pietra, I venture through a stone arch onto the graceful bridge, walking on the cobbles and admiring the bridge and river views. The place looks sublime from this traffic-free viewpoint. This is still the city of love, with amorous couples bedecking seats, statues, grassy swards, and the river banks; William Shakespeare has a lot to answer for.

I buy a bottle of water and, unusually for me, I consume it there and then; it is a hot day and all this walking is thirsty work. I make it back to the station just in time to miss the 16:02 Milan train, but another train pulls in at 16:30. On board, the guard, in perfect English, informs me that I can only ride on this train if I have a seat reservation, as the train is technically fully booked. But she says if I alight at the next stop and catch the first train after this one, then I don't have to pay any more. This little incentive makes up my mind to change trains. And I only have to wait a few minutes for a following train to take me to the junction at Brescia.

I need to use a toilet at Brescia, but there is an admission charge. I notice a small crowd on the platform, studying the locked toilet door. Then someone leaves from inside – and there is a charge as around a dozen of us squeeze through the open door into a spacious toilet area, without paying anything.

My final train up the branch line from Brescia pulls out of the bay platform at 18:00 and it is crowded with commuters and some students. I am pretty tired by now. The late sun's rays hit the water of Lake Iseo, and the small island with its ornate church is bathed in sparkling water, and the real bonus is that the concrete batching plant on the opposite shore is largely hidden in the heat haze. I almost miss my stop, and then race back to the hotel, arriving a couple of minutes past 7:30, where I join Sylvia and Janet for dinner.

Sylvia has had a good day, she tells me. She says that she walked unaided from the hotel to the centre this afternoon, and her ped count today is up to 1,880, the second highest of the week.

We end the evening drinking coffee where the tables are almost an extension of a pavement café. Janet says she wouldn't want to stay here for a long time, as there would be nothing for her to do. We suggest she could join the local socialist party, go to mass three times a week in the church with the bell tower, and get stuck into the tea dancing. Go on Janet; you know you love the tea dancing, really. Janet doesn't seem too impressed with our suggestions.

Saturday 10 June

RELAXING OVER GRISHAM

There is no rest for Sylvia on the first day of the week end. She is back in the therapy centre and on the treadmill from the outset. At least we have tomorrow off. Sylvia wears a stretch band to ensure she walks straight.

A bloke going by the name of Julio is being put through his paces, being made to walk around the outer edge of the gym. His neurotherapist is urging him to go even faster. We all feel sorry for him.

Sylvia's next task is to stretch in order to touch coloured circles on the wall; perhaps we could rig out the garage back home as a gym? There are also coloured rings on the floor, and Sylvia has to negotiate herself through them, and at the same time make her footsteps softer.

On one of the walls of this room there is a picture which gives the impression that someone has punched a hole through the masonry, revealing blue sky beyond – a graphic way of encouraging Parkinson's sufferers to punch out of the limitations of the disease and gain freedom outside its restrictions. It's a powerful message – no words, but the message is crystal clear; the picture says it all.

With the use of a camcorder, Sylvia is filmed walking; since Monday, the recording shows that the length between Sylvia's steps has increased from 38cm to 49cm. The symmetry is also a lot better. It's been a good day at the office for Sylvia.

At the end of the session, Agata tells us she is getting married in Las Vagas in a couple of weeks' time. One of the Italian ladies on the course doesn't seem to be impressed by this. "Five minutes to get married in Las Vagas and then it's five minutes to get divorced!" A little embarrassed laughter ripples around the room.

On the way out of the centre, I try to make use of my ticket discount and ask for a lower admission price to the spa, as the cost is £30. They tell me that I already have a 25% discount and that the ticket covers the Turkish bath, sauna, mud treatment, etc, but it still seems expensive to me.

After lunch, back at the hotel, Sylvia takes a turn for the worse. I walk over to the spa to see if we can use our tickets next week, and the answer is yes. Around two in the afternoon, the sound of heavy bass music permeates the hotel. The hotel manager says it's a special party to celebrate the opening of a new aqua park. I get a mental image of our son, David, at the controls of the music.

Later in the afternoon, I sit in the small patio garden by the statue of the Roman lady, with the fountain gushing forth in the background. I drink a glass of tonic water, write post cards and spend some time reading John Grisham's *Calico Joe*. I also chat to the hotel manager, Mauro, who says it's not been that good, business-wise, this year, with relatively low occupancy rates up until the last week. I ask him if he ever has a day off. "No" he says, "Not until November when the hotel closes for a month. Then I go ski-ing and rock climbing, and you don't have to go so far for these activities in November!"

Later on, Mauro advises me on taxis to get to the small lakeside town of Pisogne tomorrow, where the three of us are planning to visit. He then books a taxi for ten in the morning. It's a cheaper option than trekking to Lake Garda, especially as we don't have to meet up with Anja now.

Sylvia's ped count is 1,206.

Sunday 11 June

LAGO D'ISEO

Lake Iseo at Pisogne

Island of Loretto

We have a lazy morning, arriving in the hotel breakfast room at nine. Over breakfast we impress Mauro with the colloquial expression "super-duper" (if that's how you spell it). Mauro thinks it is quite funny, and I have no doubt that he will be repeating it to his guests during the day.

Our taxi driver collects us bang on ten and takes us to Pisogne. This delightful little settlement sits at the north-eastern end of Lake Iseo. The lakeside is refreshingly cool as we walk and push Sylvia's wheelchair along the car-free promenade. There are lots of cyclists, in all shapes and sizes. Several bikes have bambini on board, some sitting in baskets by the handlebars. One cycle is pulling a trailer with a large dog occupying it. The lake isn't short of fish, judging by the numbers swimming close to the shore.

It's a relaxed and peaceful scene on the edge of the lake, with church bells ringing, people chatting in small groups, sometimes with their dogs, and one old man engaging two Jehovah's Witnesses in conversation. The JWs give us one look, decide we are foreign and avoid us. Out in the lake, a man in a canoe barks instructions to the three junior canoeists ahead of him.

We clamber aboard the ferry that will take us to the island which I visited last Tuesday. The boat crosses the northern end of the lake and stops briefly at the town of Lovere. This town, on the opposite shore to Pisogne, has an elegant frontage of traditional housing facing the lake, reminding me of a Paris street scene. A very old hotel near the waterfront bears the title 'albergho moderno' ('modern hotel'), which strikes me as amusing.

There is a lot of housing under construction further to the south along the western shore of the lake. Many of the new homes are being carved out of the hillside, but the low rise (in the main) buildings with red roofs, following the contours, limit its impact on the character of the lake and its setting. There has been a lot of quarrying on this side of the lake; some of the quarry faces are now overgrown with extensive vegetation and they could well be valuable wildlife habitats. Some of the limestone rock faces are near vertical in their alignment, making for dramatic ravines and amazing angles of clearly defined strata.

We sail past quite a lot of floating real estate which is going nowhere fast and people sunning themselves across the decks of yachts and speedboats. There are even a few sailing boats making use of the breeze, plying up and down the lake. I photograph two adult swans taking their five cygnets out for a Sunday morning swim. There is a healthy feeling of peaceful coexistence on the lake.

The ferry lands at the village of Carzano on the main island in the lake – Monte Isola - at 12:30. It's really hot just inshore from the lake, and we push Sylvia in her wheelchair along several narrow passages through the small traffic-free village (with the exception of a few mopeds). At the end of the built-up area we come across a public park with lots of people sunbathing. Finding a shady bench, we consume our packed lunch, which the hotel has provided for us. It's a perfect time to read and relax.

We make our way back to the landing station to wait for our return ferry to Pisogne. This ferry is advertised on the real-time electronic information board as departing at 15:05 hrs. But 15:05 comes and goes with no ferry in sight. Then the details of the Pisogne ferry disappear from the screen. A slight panic sets in, but the locals reassure me that the ferry is coming, and it finally arrives about 15 minutes late; quite respectable timekeeping when compared to many British train operating companies.

Moving back up the lake is pleasantly cool and invigorating; it's worth taking the ferry just to cool down, irrespective of whether one is going to a destination. There are so many pleasure craft that I wonder whether the lake is near to reaching its capacity. In addition to the boats, there are quite a few paragliders, which make for colourful sight.

People are generally positive with helping us move Sylvia in her wheelchair. The chivalrous ferry captain personally carries it off the boat when we land at Pisogne. We decide to celebrate our arrival at Pisogne with ice cream and soft drinks, and I order them before attempting to ring our friendly taxi driver from this morning, who said earlier that he was happy to collect us and drive us home. But I can't get through to him on my mobile; another potential panic. I ask for advice in a nearby bar, and they ring the taxi number on their phone and let me speak to him.

Our taxi driver collects us just after I photograph a train passing through a level crossing, a few metres from our pavement café. The bar which helps me with the phone call offers at least 50 flavours of ice cream, and in the end I opt for 'melone verde' ('green melon') which doesn't disappoint. It's all very agreeable and the ladies give me the impression that they have enjoyed themselves in quite a restful sort of way.

We are driven back to our hotel to the strains of Witney Houston. We discover this evening that we have something else in common with Mauro. In conversation with him, I say: "no problem", to which he replies: "hakuna matatu". My eyes light up and I ask him:" Do you know what language that is?", and he replies: "ki swahili". It transpires that he has visited Kenya eight times and has picked up a few Swahili expressions. It's a small world, as we lived and worked in Kenya in the 1970s.

Sylvia's ped count is 1,515 steps.

Monday 12 June

SYLVIA IS PUSHED VERY HARD

We are now into week 2 of our course at the European Parkinson's Therapy Centre. By 09:30, Sylvia is in action with her walking and cycling exercises, but this time she is pushed for ten minutes on each activity instead of the usual five minutes.

Other English people arrive at the centre this morning. A couple from London introduce themselves. The husband says he is a 'drug dealer', which initially raises eyebrows until it is further explained that he supplies drugs to the NHS. His wife has Parkinson's, and she appears to be struggling with it. Also, there is a student called Marnie from Oxford Brookes University, studying nutrition. She is out here for two months, working on her dissertation, which goes under a long title. Even she can't remember the title exactly, but she brings it up on her mobile and it's at least three lines long, but in essence appears to be about the relationship of diet to Parkinson's.

Later in the morning we are introduced to Louise, a podiatrist (foot specialist), who takes a number of measurements of Sylvia's feet and says she will get back to us later in the week with recommended insoles for her.

Then, finally, we meet Alex, who is the Director of the centre and who happens to be British. He also has Parkinson's disease. We didn't meet him last week, as he was in hospital undergoing treatment for his condition, involving the use of electrodes in his brain (deep brain stimulation or DBS). He says that they placed the electrodes too deeply and the issue is not resolved yet.

Janet asks him about any future plans he may have for his work with Parkinson's therapy. Alex explains that the centre, working with Parkinson's UK, have opened a centre near Oxford for newly diagnosed patients and they are currently rolling out 6 more centres with the aim of having 24 by 2019. His plans seem quite ambitious to me. However, the Managing Director of Parkinson's UK is backing the project and they have regular visits from Parkinson's UK directors and personnel. An important moment came when he had a meeting lined up with David Cameron to secure UK funding for this work. On the way from London Heathrow Airport to number 10 Downing Street, a message came up on his mobile – "Cameron resigns". So near and yet so far.....but contact with the government goes on.

Alex speaks about the Italian medical scene, where in his view there is an attitude in some quarters that they don't really welcome competition, for example to their established way of thinking.

After lunch, I walk to the local tourism office and add to my collection of maps. Then the lady in the next door newsagent's cheers me up by saying that British newspapers will be delivered tomorrow.

We go back to the centre at 5 pm to hear a presentation by Alex. One of Alex's introductory statements goes along the following lines: " For those who are Christians and believe in creative design, it follows that the human body is built to work properly through intelligent design." Then, to prove a point about the way we walk, Alex 'volunteers' me to pace up and down the room.

He then talks about the potential for re-wiring our brains; they can be modelled by new habits and disciplines. These include concentration, application, collaboration, patience and the avoidance of stress. We are encouraged to train ourselves in these areas all day long. Mechanisms to protect our brain cells from damage, including through exercise – which Alex calls neuroprotection – can produce dopamine, he says. One key way of helping to achieve this is through high intensity stretching, and that it is important to have a goal and to push yourself.

We are warned that exercising the wrong way could damage our posture and gait. "Always use your concentration" he says "and apply what you learn to avoid reinforcing the negative aspects".

Movement is clearly fundamental for both neuroplasticity and neuroprotection. The four sets of power movements – power-up, power-twist, power-rock and power-step – form the basis of the regular exercises which are promoted at the centre. These exercises, according to Alex, combat the worst-case scenarios of Parkinson's, and we are encouraged to "think big". They are a way of saying "I refuse to droop down!" Alex is clearly both highly motivated and motivational, and I for one come away at the end of the session encouraged by him.

After dinner, we walk into the thermal park gardens and sit well away from the music. Four ducks, in single file, cross over the path near our park bench and push their way through the bushes where they peck at the grass. After some apparent and fairly noisy confusion, they all succeed in finding the gap in the hedge through which they entered the grassy area and beat a retreat.

We walk back towards the hotel, past the music, which is more of an "oompah, oompah, stick it up your jumpa" variety. It's still quite warm at 9:30 as we walk back to the hotel but the streets are quiet and it's very peaceful. Sylvia has achieved 1,876 steps on her pedometer today.

Tuesday 13 June
LAKE MORO

Lake Moro

Sylvia and Kathy

It has been a hot and sticky night and neither of us slept a lot. In fact, Sylvia says that she didn't sleep at all. I think it is time to kick-start the air conditioning in our bedroom.

This morning's session with Agata is hard for Sylvia. The knee exercises are a killer for her, not helped by sleep loss from last night, and she almost gives up for the day. But after a trip to the bathroom she agrees to attempt the cycling exercise, provided she can do it to music, and she says something like Michael Jackson will do; she settles for the music of Billy Joel and gets through the session in one piece.

Alex offers to take a small group of us up to Lake Moro at 3:30 this afternoon. A recently arrived lady by the name of Kathy, from Ireland, says she wants to swim in the lake. Despite her invitation, I don't think I will follow her example.

In the early afternoon I walk to the friendly bookshop where I was told there would be a British newspaper today. True enough, I find The Times, but it is last Friday's edition, the day after the UK General Election. It costs 4 euros, but the lure of reading a paper in English is too much to resist. I learn that the value of the UK pound has fallen further, inflation has started to rise, and the UK has recorded the lowest growth rate in Europe over the last six months, plus there has been a 96% drop in nurses coming to the UK from the rest of Europe – further results of the dog's dinner aka Brexit. Will the hung parliament we now have after the election lead to a softer Brexit? Maybe there's more to play for, now Mrs May doesn't have the landslide she was anticipating.

Just after three in the afternoon, Alex piles us into his people carrier, which he tells us is a donation from government funding (36,000 euros, but they still have to pay back 12,000 euros). We are a small party of six (plus Alex). Kathy is Irish and looks far too fit and young to have Parkinson's; she is married to a German, lives in Frankfurt and she has two teenage kids (Ciara and Connor). A couple, David and Mary, are also Irish, from near Dublin, and I would say they are around our age. A few months ago Mary suffered a bad fall, which is quite common for people with Parkinson's symptoms. This has affected her confidence and her head droops most of the time. David is a part time psychotherapist with links to the Tavistock Institute. The other member of our group is Sylvia's sister, Janet.

Alex drives us along a narrow road which climbs up away from the valley floor in a series of hair-pin bends, which scare the living daylights out of me, but Alex is an experienced driver. At the top, the track levels out and we park by a small, traditional and beautiful church (Santa Apollonia), which has an even more beautiful interior. A footpath leads us beyond the church. And then, through a gap in the reeds, there it is. Lake Moro's dark blue waters are contained in a verdant, upland bowl, and the lake is stunningly beautiful.

Even at 4pm on a week day, the grassy slopes around the lake are populated by scores of people, mostly below the age of 20, plus a few dogs. Kathy decides to go for a swim in the lake, and says the water is fresh and relaxing. I tell her that I believe her, but I'm not about to prove it for myself. Sylvia invites Mary to sit in her wheelchair, whilst David buys us all cold drinks from a nearby café.

David and I then go for a short stroll to try and find a viewpoint looking over the Camonica Valley, which starts life in Switzerland. Darfo, the next door neighbour to Boario Terme, and makes up the other half of the combined settlement, can clearly be seen a few hundred feet below us. It's quite a bit cooler up here on a clear and sunny afternoon. We come across a smallholder, scything his grass in the traditional way; time has stood still in this little corner of Italy. After shouting to ask his permission to take a photograph of him, we get no response, so our cameras go 'click' very suddenly, and then we move away, sharpish.

I walk alone along the edge of the lake on a rough path. On the opposite shore, there is much evidence of terracing on the hillsides, to make way for a few houses and smallholdings. But they don't seem out of place in the landscape.

Half an hour later, Alex drives us all back to our hotels. Dave asks Alex the question that is probably in all our minds – "How did you find yourself living and working in Italy, seeing as you are British?" The answer comes back – "Love". Alex goes on to explain that he saw a girl on a beach (I think he says in Corfu) and that he knew instantly that she was the one for him. Apparently, she wasn't as sure as he was at first (which I for one think was perfectly understandable), but he says, that when she was in the UK studying, he took her to Guernsey, one of the Channel Islands, and he then says she was smitten; he omits to say whether she was smitten with him or with Guernsey, but the rest is history. They have been married some time and have a family, and he admits to being very settled out here.

I can't resist the follow-up question – "Do you think your meeting with your future wife was a chance encounter?" Alex replies – "No, as a Christian, I believe God led me to my wife". The road journey back to Boario Terme isn't long enough to tease out more details, but Alex does go on to say as we leave the mountainous track and drive into the town that he is an elder in a small fellowship which started life as part of a Pentecostal church. He tells us that he is also involved with Oak Hall, a Christian tour company, and he is their North Italian logistics guy. They have holidays in Tuscany and Sicily planned for later in the year.

We invite the others round to our hotel for drinks at 8:30 this evening and then rest up in our bedroom for about an hour with the air conditioning full on. After yet another wonderful meal in our hotel, which includes fresh pineapple and cream, we stay on for the performance of Emilio and Barbara playing the accordion and singalong – except only Emilio shows up.

One of the elderly lady guests in the hotel asks me if I can dance. I'm afraid I say "no". "Why?" she asks, and I say that I am too old, which seems to amuse her, possibly on account of my very bad Italian, which must be grammatically atrocious. She gives me a playful pat on my arm, but mercifully she doesn't persist.

Sylvia's ped count is down to 918; I start reading Sebastian Faulks' novel *A Week in December*. It doesn't take long to fall asleep tonight.

MIKE TAKES THE WATERS

Sylvia has had a good night's sleep and the air conditioning is wonderful. This morning I take the plunge, as it were, and indulge in the local spa, which has put Boario Terme on the map. I'm like 'little boy lost' to begin with, but several young ladies take me by the hand and show the various relevant parts of the spa. There are a series of indoor pools at different levels, the lowest of which flows out into an outdoor pool, where the water temperature drops markedly (perhaps not surprisingly). One of the pools has what looks like a shower head and a button; I press it and a surge of water strikes me with the force of a jet engine, and I almost lose my balance.

Another facility is a bed-shaped feature under the water for one to lie on. Then, at the touch of a button, water spurts from underneath my body, as a force of stimulation. At this point I find it difficult, in a state of lying in the horizontal, to actually move off the bed. The brain is telling me one thing and the body is not responding. This could be the nearest I am ever going to get to the experience of freezing that many Parkinson's sufferers, including Sylvia, undergo on a quasi-regular basis.

I survive the aquatic experience and meet up with Sylvia and Janet mid-morning, where we join David from Ireland for a drink of coffee in the small café at the entrance to the spa. He says that he is aware of new developments in relation to the freezing that people with the Parkinson's condition experience. He takes down our e-mail details so he can pass on this information. Sylvia says she has just collected her new insoles to help her walk better.

After a restful afternoon, we return to the centre at around six for a presentation on stress, or anti-stress, by Daria, one of the therapists. Her message has several key points. Firstly, Parkinson's symptoms get worse when stress is experienced. Secondly, techniques for 'resetting' your psyche include breathing, and this is so important that we need to stop and take time to do this properly. Apparently, when we are anxious, the frequency of our breathing increases, and we can't get enough oxygen. Then the mind is affected. "We should try to take deeper breaths", says Daria, "then the muscles relax. Stiffness is a symptom of your problems. Also, shaking should improve. The aim is to relax the mind, which is very powerful. The main muscle to breathe deeper is the diaphragm. Practising is very important".

In a question and answer session, she says that the jury is out on the question of whether stress causes the onset of Parkinson's or whether stress is a symptom of Parkinson's; research is ongoing. "But we do know", she says, "that dopamine is involved in our emotions". But what is also clear is that we can learn to relax better and that breathing exercises are important.

It's now time to put some of the breathing theory into practice. Daria says: "Get into a comfortable position, with your legs apart. Breathe through your nose, and exhale through your mouth. Feel your belly. Then breathe deeper, close your eyes and think of a favourite place and colour. Raise and lower your hands. One of the best moments to do this is when we lie down in bed before we fall asleep". Daria tells us that we should keep practising during the day, just five minutes at a time, and that yawning is OK by the way.

Sylvia and Janet reckon I fall asleep at this point. What? Me! This can't possibly be true! We thank Daria and head out into street.

Thunder and dark clouds hang over the town of Boario Terme in the early evening as we leave the centre and make our way back to the hotel. Rain is imminent. I push Sylvia in the wheelchair as fast as I can and we just make it to the hotel before the inevitable downpour. The heavy rain lasts a long time. It is the perfect opportunity to write a few postcards, something I enjoy doing. Sylvia's ped count is 893.

Leonora, the hotel manager's daughter, has taken to calling Sylvia 'Lady Sylvia'. She is getting quite in tune with Sylvia's dietary needs, such as minimal protein and concentrating on carbohydrates. In contrast, I am probably eating too much of everything; but 'everything' is so well presented and delicious. And I can't remember a hotel where the staff are so attentive to the customers' needs and are so pleasant to relate to.

After our meal, we take coffee in the hotel lounge. We are clearly in reflective mood and the three of us discuss a number of topics, not all obviously related, including (1) the economic impact of Brexit; (2) when you hear so much about fake news, whether you can trust the media, including the Times newspaper; and (3) the appropriateness of dance in Christian worship. I think my views are – (1) disastrous if we end up with a hard Brexit; (2) generally trustworthy, but everyone makes mistakes from time to time; and (3) generally appropriate if done sensitively. Finally, we are all in agreement on the inappropriateness of the use of mobile phones in restaurants, something that would feature in my Room 101 list (and Janet's).

It's been raining all evening, but interestingly, the fountain in the courtyard only gets turned off at ten tonight.

LIVING WITH PARKINSON'S

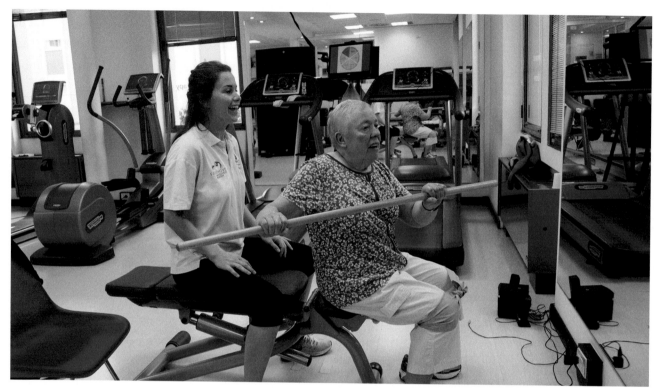

Approach ramming speed!

Relaxing in a local café

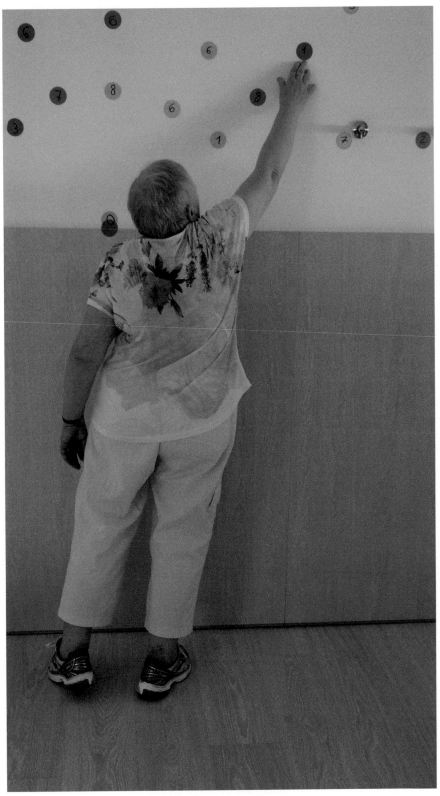

Stretching is good for you

It's scientific as well as physical

Relaxing in the hotel patio garden

Alex the Director of the Centre and Sylvia

David and Mary

'The day starts with a mini-crisis. I can't find my wallet and eventually I call the hotel. The staff go into overdrive, searching everywhere. One of the staff finds it in the bathroom; I find this very embarrassing.

The programme for the day at the centre starts with exercises using the wall bar. There's a lot of lifting of arms and legs, transferring weight from one leg to the other, and attempting to reach coloured spots on the wall; a technicolour version of hell. Then Sylvia has to hold her foot in the air for five seconds, then ten, and repeat it five times. "Pay attention, Sylvia!" encourages Agata, "Put your left hand on the wall, put your weight on your right leg; squeeze your right bottom; then lift your left leg." Then Sylvia is exhorted to join all these exercises together into continuous walking. Agata says Sylvia has worked hard this morning, and she takes a video on my mobile to prove it.

At this point David and Mary enter and we get talking. Mary says that she had a fall in her home at Christmas and suffered whiplash. Her head falls down unless she props it up with her hand. She also says she is looking forward to going back to her book club in Ireland.

It's time to settle our accounts with the centre. I pay the bill on my visa card. Sara organises the administration; she is smilingly efficient, and her English is excellent. Sara asks where I am from, and when I say I come from Torquay, which is by the sea, her eyes light up. I tell her that if she is ever visiting England, she is welcome to visit us.

Back at the hotel we have drinks on the terrace, facing the street. A Nigerian guy engages us in conversation and sells me some handkerchiefs. He says he's been over here for eight years, but he is still searching for a regular job. I wonder if the problem is about to get worse for him, with the increased competition from thousands of new arrivals hitting the Italian shores and boundaries in search of work or just to escape hardship, war and persecution. Our new Nigerian friend is very chatty. I say two words in Italian and he congratulates me on my fluency (!) and shakes my hand. I have no idea how accommodating to young Africans the Italian public are, but this lad certainly has charm and he strikes me as being a survivor. I hope he lands a permanent job soon.

After lunch, we attempt to walk off our food by going on a circular walk, which initially follows the railway, in the direction of Darfo, Boario Terme's twin town which joins it to the south. At Darfo Station, a cycle path takes us over the River Oglio, which looks dangerous to swim in, judging by the strong currents and masses of slimy green vegetation, just below the level of the water. But this is not deterring local children from splashing around in the river below the bridge.

Just beyond a football ground we come onto a newly constructed road, which enables us to re-cross the same river on a new (dating from 2013), utilitarian-looking, girder bridge. We are now walking through agricultural land which looks intensively cultivated, including a rice crop, although a few horses graze in one field. Maybe development will follow the new road in due course, but for now it is a rural scene with a few roofs of houses in the middle distance across the fields.

Half an hour later we are back in the hotel, drinking cold orangeade before cooling off in the shower.

Later in the afternoon we walk through the rain to the centre for a presentation by Alex on the subject of living with Parkinson's. He says it is 200 years since an English guy called James Parkinson discovered the condition. He says: "Many people don't know the truth about Parkinson's or how to live with it".

We are told that it is almost as though there were several cooks, serving different dishes from different ingredients. The first set is termed the motor symptoms; for some people, it's about tremor, for others it's about posture and yet for others it's about stride length. Other symptoms in this set can include slowness of movement or even difficulty in moving at all, back pain, poor balance, cramp and lack of co-ordination.

Just to complicate the mix, excess of dopamine through inappropriate medication can also unnecessarily bring on these symptoms. However, Alex explains that all of the above symptoms respond to neuro therapy, even tremor, which is perhaps the greatest challenge.

We then consider a number of what Alex terms 'non-motor' symptoms, and there are quite a few of these. They include tiredness, constipation, swollen ankles, difficulties in swallowing, changes in blood pressure, sleep problems, acid reflux, loss of the sense of smell, loss of voice, sore eyes, sudden sleep, increased sexual activity, increased tension, difficulty in writing and dermatitis.

A symptom common to most Parkinson's sufferers is MCI – mild cognitive impairment – which involves the freezing of gait – but interestingly, people don't freeze on stairs, where there a lines to cross, such as steps. Research has shown that lines on the floor decrease blocking/freezing by 80%.

Alex says: "Of course, it is quite common for 'normal' people to experience a number of these problems, but Parkinson's sufferers experience several together, and the combinations can be critical". He now moves on to the final set of symptoms, which are psychological. "These are often the worst", he says. The set includes apathy, depression, fear and anxiety. "Look out for them" Alex says and he then advises: "The best therapy for Parkinson's is living and getting on with life, and not giving up". One lesson to learn is to focus on quality rather than quantity - we are on the slow train now, so let's enjoy the view! We also need to know ourselves better, as a famous Greek philosopher once said.

At this point, Alex circulates papers to all the Parkinson's people in the room. "I want you to write down ten things you would like to do; I'm looking for some passion – things that make your life count". He then identifies three things that really help us on the slow train. They are (i) doing DIY; (ii) doing something creative, such as writing a book; and (iii) in giving, you receive. We are also encouraged to learn new things, such as taking up a musical instrument or learning a new language. Alex says that the biggest road block in our lives is us! And it's a lie to think that we are not worth anything.

At the end of the presentation, an Italian in the group by the name of Angelo says in English: "I am very boring in my hotel". We then realise that he is saying that he is bored in his hotel! It's a common linguistic error made by many trying to come to terms with the English language. Angelo then tells us that he has booked a table in a restaurant – and can we all join him this evening? Unfortunately, the rest of us have all made arrangements with our hotels for this evening's meal and no one is able to join him. It's a sad situation, but it's too short notice, and it wouldn't be fair on our hotel if we cancelled our meals at this late hour.

We come away from the centre, thinking about the ten things that we would really like to do. Janet reckons throwing the ball for our dog Katy is on her list (it would certainly be on Katy's top ten list), and we agree that some of the simplest things in life are the most satisfying.

Sylvia's ped count is 904.

Friday 16 June

SYLVIA'S FINAL DAY IN THE TORTURE CHAMBER

The sound of boy racers on their scooters pierces through the peaceful atmosphere of this small town somewhere around the hour of six; this is something that is definitely not on my top ten list of things to do. Before breakfast, Sylvia completes her form from yesterday evening's session, writing out her ten most enjoyable things to do.

The first session this morning at the centre is an assessment for Sylvia with Silvia, her psychotherapist. After we return home, back to the UK that is, we are to make contact with the centre on 2 July and also go out for a meal together, just the two of us. I can cope with this.

It's now time for Sylvia's last 'torture' session with Agata. Firstly, Sylvia goes through a number of boxing moves, complete with the proper gloves. I get volunteered to spar with her and quickly realise that I was sensible not to pursue boxing as my day job.

Sylvia then goes through the power exercise routine, to the accompaniment of the Spice Girls. "Very good, Sylvia!" shouts Agata. At the end of all this exercise we bump into another couple we have got to know a little, a Jewish man and wife from London, going by the names of John and Frances. They tell us they have just celebrated 50 years of marriage. "The secret to a long marriage is very simple", John says, "it's all about trust and understanding; she doesn't trust me and I don't understand her!"

We bump into David and Mary – and immediately notice a transformation in Mary's posture. She is looking at us, head held high with no need to use her hands. Back in Ireland, friends have been massaging the back of her neck, but here at the centre, they have been massaging the front of her neck, and this has made all the difference. A simple point perhaps, but the changed approach has been radical for Mary. This is a great good news story.

Sylvia then receives an assessment from Silvia, the psychotherapist; she says she is pleased with Sylvia, and she has made progress in relation to all four pillars.

In the very hot early afternoon, I do a silly thing and push Sylvia in her wheelchair towards the 'Archaeo - Park'. It is really hot, probably in the mid-thirties Celsius and there is no shade. Before too long, I decide to turn back. I reckon by now I could be an Olympic wheelchair pusher.

Alex gives us a presentation at the centre at four in the afternoon, starting with diet. "We need the right diet", he says by way of introduction, to which none of us can really disagree. "We should be aiming to maintain a BMI (body mass index) of around 18-25". (But it's no use telling us this now, Alex, after the wonderful hotel you put us in.) Some of Alex's tips include: (i) limit your intake of red meat and milk products; (ii) eat fish and beans as a protein source; (iii) drink lots of water; and (iv) periodic fasting may be helpful.

He then refers to three classic problems affecting Parkinson's sufferers. The first is constipation and Alex's suggestions are to limit the use of laxatives and to drink two litres of water per day, which should be treated as medicine; and use herbal remedies where possible. The second problem is acid reflux, and Alex's suggestion is to sleep at least three hours after eating. The third problem is dysphagia, which affects many Parkinson's patients that he deals with.

Finally, on the subject of diet, Alex has a few more words of advice: (i) never take levodopa with food; (ii) avoid protein at lunch time, and keep to salads, etc; (iii) there is little evidence that supplements can be a game changer; and (iv) it is impossible to have just one Parkinson's diet which fits everyone's needs.

Alex now turns his attention to medicine, which is the first of the four pillars for combatting Parkinson's. His opening shots are: "The best medicine you can take is to carry on living", and: "Take the least amount of medicine you possibly can". Alex has just been treated with what is termed 'Deep Brain Stimulation (DBS), which has reduced his medicine intake by 60%, but he also advises that 1% of DBS operations go wrong. Alex then runs through a list of the main groups of medicines for people affected by Parkinson's.

Research is currently ongoing into stem cell application, although Alex seems cautious about some of the claims for a cure. An approach called Terapia Genetica is being developed at Oxford, and initial signs are promising. Another area of research based on cell repair is being developed in New Zealand, whilst ultrasound research could be fast-tracked in the next two years. So there is quite a lot going on.

Silvia then gives us a presentation on cognitive therapy. She explains that we all experience cognitive problems as we age, but we also experience selective recall – and to prove this she plays us a short video. Our task is to concentrate on a game of basketball and we are asked to remember exactly how many times the white team pass the ball. After watching the film for five minutes and concentrating very hard, we all say what we thought the figure was, with our answers covering a range of around 12-15 passes. Silvia than asks us what else did we notice in the film. "We noticed the black team" we all say. "Anything else?" she asks. We all draw a blank. "What about the guerrilla?" "What guerrilla?" we all say incredulously. Silvia re-runs the same film and there it is – there is someone in a guerrilla outfit right in the thick of the basketball game, for the entire video, really in your face, as it were. None of us saw the guerrilla first time round.

Silvia says this illustrates how selective our attention span is, and neuroplasticity is all about training our mind to concentrate on new and more beneficial things. This can help us to overcome cognitive problems, and training is important. It is important to be active, and in this environment, the brain improves. "Learn something new" Silvia says, "this is important for your mood and for your psychological life". She says that depression is common with Parkinson's sufferers and she develops the concept of the slow train, with the help of a short video. The Slow Train Video informs us that with Parkinson's you are no longer on the fast train, the bullet train or TGV. Instead, we are now on the slow train, and a lovely picture of a steam train comes across the screen. Now we have different views, in fact we can see more and we need to colour our life.

My only negative comment about this evening is that we have been faced with information overload; there has been a lot to take in, although to be fair, there has been time to ask questions and discuss. And it is all so interesting.

After our evening meal I take a photograph of the lady who calls herself 'Mama', together with Eleanora and Mauro (her daughter and son), behind the bar. They want copies and give me their e-mail to make sure I do it; I now have no excuse.

Janet, Sylvia and I meet up with Angelo from our course for a late night drink at the hotel. Angelo has been on the course for a week. Despite his low opinion of his standard of English, he converses well, and his political knowledge of the UK is impressive. He says that the ultimate thing he really wants to do in life is visit Machu Picchu in Peru, although he says that in his condition the five day donkey trek from Cuzco would probably take him fifteen days. We raise our glasses and drink to Angelo and Machu Picchu.

Sylvia's ped count is 1,569.

Saturday 17 June
SLOW TRAIN TO EDOLO

Mauro, Elenora and 'Mama' at Hotel Diana

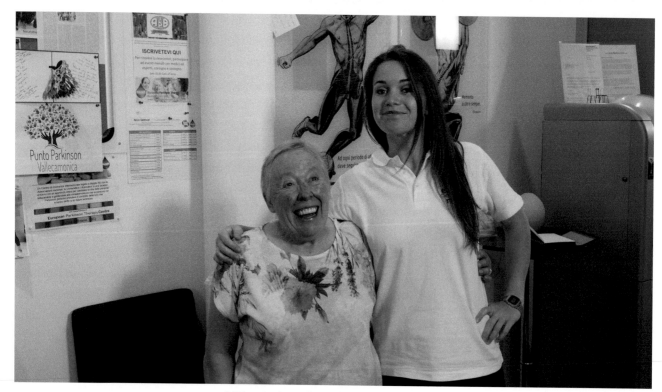

Ultimate bonding: Sylvia and Agata

Alex and David

Is Sylvia finally enjoying it?

Sylvia, Mike and Angelo at Hotel Diana

Vale Camonica

Edolo – end of the line

It is Sylvia's final test day at the centre. Sylvia repeats the six minutes' walking test in the gym. On the first day of the course, she walked for 152 metres; today she covers 335 metres over the same time (with the aid of a 'flash mob' song called *Every Praise*, directed by Hezekiah Walker), which is a clear signal as to how far she has come in two weeks. She covers 25 laps compared with 11.7 laps two weeks ago.

Just to bring us back to reality, Sylvia freezes the next time she tries to walk. Agata says that there is something wrong, and that Sylvia must see the Parkinson's nurse back home. She comments that the freezing seems to occur at about the same time every morning.

It's time for a few farewells. A student from Oxford Brookes University called Marnie, who has been a friendly face all week, says goodbye, and Melana, one of the physios takes a photograph of us. Alex comes into the room, asks Sylvia to stand up and then gives her a hug, which I think catches her by surprise.

In the late morning, Sylvia and I go shopping, based on an unguarded comment that I would buy her a handbag. We locate one in a friendly shop opposite the hotel. Janet thinks the bag is too big and says that Sylvia will never find anything now; she's probably right.

After lunch, a couple in the hotel from Turin come over to us and tell us they are leaving and say goodbye; a nice touch.

In the afternoon, Sylvia and I, in the spirit of the Parkinson's therapy advice, take the slow train to the end of the line at Edolo, not far from the Swiss border. The train – definitely a slow train - wends its way up the valley for about an hour, and the scenery takes on more of an Alpine feel. The mountains have more snow resting in the gulleys near the peaks. There are several hydro-electric power (HEP) schemes with their tunnels bringing the water to the valley floor, which gets progressively narrower as our train fights the uphill gradient. We pass through some tunnels and in places the track hugs steeply sloping and near-vertical rock faces. The swift flowing headwaters of the Oglio River empty into Lake Iseo way down the valley.

Several prominent church towers dominate the small towns and villages that we pass as our journey continues to twist and turn uphill. A couple of dams are holding back the waters of the Oglio River, linked to the HEP schemes. There is some heavy industry, including forges and stone cutting, nestling in the valley floor, occupying the limited flat spaces which are at a premium.

Edolo is the small settlement at the end of the line; there are a few sidings and the final buffers. There's little traffic in the main street as we make our way from the station. But it offers great views of the surrounding mountains, with terraced farms on some of the lower slopes.

There's time for a drink in a friendly bar before catching the next train back, half an hour later. We almost have the train to ourselves, the total sum of fellow travellers being two cyclists and four English tourists who sound like they come from a long way north of Watford; although we are not really listening to them, the sound of their conversation carries through the nearly empty carriage. They become embroiled in a conversation about why there is a hierarchy in the Catholic Church. "What's the point?" asks one of the men in the group. "If Jesus was here today, he would ..." – at which point the train enters a tunnel and I will never know the answer to this key theological question...

Although there's a lot of electricity generated in the valley, there are no wind turbines that I can make out from the train. Despite the industry, much of it heavy, the valley still largely retains its beauty, especially in its narrowest sections, where the streams are youthful and mountainous crags loom ever closer to the train. It almost free-wheels through progressively lower altitudes back to Boario Terme, where we alight at four in the afternoon.

Once back in the hotel, we text Janet to let her know where we are. I consume a cold drink, take a shower, pack most of my bag for the journey tomorrow, and then retire to the courtyard to read some Sebastian Faulks.

Later in the afternoon, our hotel is 'overrun' by a lot of exuberant young ladies. Mauro on reception tells me they are from ladies' football teams who tomorrow will be playing in a national final of small teams from all over Italy.

After dinner, we enjoy a brass band performing in the street, just outside the hotel; a pleasant way to end the day.

Sylvia's ped count is 1,816.

THE TREK HOME

We say our final goodbyes at the hotel; we have been looked after very well-almost too well; how will I measure on the bathroom scales tomorrow?

Our airport taxi collects us, and the initial part of the journey is fine and uneventful, apart from going through some long tunnels. Sylvia isn't a great fan of tunnels, which is unfortunate, as there are 15 of them, some several miles long. But at a roundabout, the carabinieri are blocking the road which we need to take to the airport. (All we are told is that there is an incident and the road will be closed for at least two hours). We are forced to find an alternative route, back through the same set of tunnels (deep joy for Sylvia).

At Bergamo airport, finding a trolley is like seeking gold dust, and it takes some time before I spot an abandoned one. (Well, I hope it was abandoned). The airport departure area is very crowded. We also discover that we have little time to catch our flight, which takes off at 11:50 hrs, which is less than an hour after we arrived at the airport. Having Sylvia with us in a wheelchair is a clear advantage in helping us gain rapid access to the departure gate.

The plane takes off over the North Italian countryside; small towns and scattered villages hold hands across fertile fields. Soon we are over the Alps – I never tire of looking at the ice-clad peaks, including a couple of glaciers.

We are seated at the front of the aircraft. Even trying to drink a small can of coke is an adventure in the small space available. Sylvia passes to me her empty can, except that it's not empty and I am wearing a pair of wet trousers to prove it.

There are clear views of what I assume is the Black Forest, where there is a pattern of islands of fields, pasture land and small villages within a sea of dark green woodland, stretching for miles and miles. Slight turbulence greets us as we cross the North Sea.

At Stansted Airport, a chatty taxi driver transports us to our parked car at the airport lodge. Britain is experiencing a heat wave – 31.5 degrees Celsius here in Essex – and there is a clear blue sky as we drive home. In the car, we have one invigorated Sylvia who is determined to carry on where she left off at the centre. I too hope to benefit from all the exercises we were taught.

It would not surprise me if we revisit Boario Terme at some point in the future.

Printed in the United States
By Bookmasters